Fixing America:
Essays on Domestic and Foreign Policy

James Matthew Sawatzki

BookLocker
Trenton, Georgia

Print ISBN: 978-1-958877-50-0
E-book ISBN: 979-8-88531-322-3

Published by BookLocker.com, Inc., Trenton, Georgia.

Library of Congress Cataloguing in Publication Data
Sawatzki, James Matthew
Fixing America: Essays on Domestic and Foreign Policy by
James Matthew Sawatzki
Library of Congress Control Number: 2022915550

BookLocker.com, Inc.
2024

First Edition

DISCLAIMER

The author and publisher are providing this book and its contents on an "as is" basis and make no representations or warranties of any kind with respect to this book or its contents. The author and publisher disclaim all such representations and warranties, including for example warranties of merchantability and advice for a particular purpose. In addition, the author and publisher do not represent or warrant that the information accessible via this book is accurate, complete or current.

The statements made about products and services have not been evaluated by the U.S. government. Please consult with your own legal, accounting, medical, or other licensed professional regarding the suggestions and recommendations made in this book.

Except as specifically stated in this book, neither the author or publisher, nor any authors, contributors, or other representatives will be liable for damages arising out of or in connection with the use of this book. This is a comprehensive limitation of liability that applies to all damages of any kind, including (without limitation) compensatory; direct, indirect or consequential damages; loss of data, income or profit; loss of or damage to property and claims of third parties.

You understand that this book is not intended as a substitute for consultation with a licensed medical, legal or accounting professional. Before you begin any change your lifestyle in any way, you will consult a licensed professional to ensure that you are doing what's best for your situation.

This book provides content related to political topics. As such, use of this book implies your acceptance of this disclaimer.

Contents

Introduction

"Why don't you write a book, Mr. Sawatzki?" was the most common question asked during my thirty-eight-year teaching career. This was closely followed by, "Why aren't you teaching in college?" and finally, "Why aren't you president of the United States?" The third one is easy; I didn't want to get divorced. There are political wives, like Hillary Clinton, and there are nonpolitical wives like Michelle Obama.

Many political wives are second or third wives. They live for the limelight nearly as much as their career husbands. Bill Clinton was in constant campaign mode when he wasn't engaged in a sexual tryst. He may have been campaigning then also. I'm sure his mistresses voted for him, as long as they were a "couple." Hillary continued to vote for him, even after his multiple affairs were exposed — which was inevitable — as they were open secrets among the national media and the Arkansas State Patrol.

I did try my hand at politics during my twenties (a late start by most standards) because I was raised in a very conservative small town in southeast Washington state. It is now referred to as Napa Valley north, and had the industry developed a little earlier, I may never have left town. House Speaker Tom Foley was from my neck of the woods — home to practical farm people, distrustful of politics, who just want to be left alone. My father was active in the local Republican Party. During my youth I attended local Catholic schools. Dad was an insurance general agent for Mutual and United of Omaha, having transported the family to Walla Walla, Washington from Omaha, Nebraska.

My earliest political memory involves traveling the back roads of Walla Walla County in a station wagon full of political signs supporting Barry Goldwater for president in 1964 and pulling over every mile or so. I held the sticks while my dad used a sledgehammer to place them. An early indication of his Libertarian politics.

I didn't want to go to college. I wanted to write for the local daily newspaper. They had already published a couple of my stories, but the local editor turned down my offer to be Jimmy Olsen and start with the obituaries and high school sports beat. He said I had to go to college to learn important things essential to my development, although he was quite vague about what those were exactly.

Saint Martin's College (now University) was the only college that recruited at my school, and they offered me an "activities scholarship." I also got one for having a Polish surname. The college is Catholic, so my mom was happy, and I filled out all the FAFSA forms (in longhand on paper) and pestered my father until he signed them. Essentially, I attended college with grants, scholarships and borrowed money. It was an excellent investment, but I was not aware of it at the time.

Being part of the "Woodward and Bernstein generation," as an Olympia, Washington editor called us, created youths of political idealism and passion for justice. Sadly, being from a small town, and without excellent high school counseling, I went to the wrong school to become a journalist. I learned close to college graduation that I should have attend a university with a daily paper in order to have any chance of a career in the news business. I would have to write for it for several years, serve as editor for at least one year and start in some Podunk town in the hinterlands to work my way up.

But I did meet a mentor, who changed my life for the better, and inspired my learning for life: Dr. Michael Contris, emeritus editor of the *Daily Olympian* and professor of humanities, who studied at the University of Chicago under Mortimer Adler (he of the 102 Great Ideas). The one thing I knew the day I arrived on campus was that I couldn't wait for my parents to vacate back home. My father was more than willing to glad-hand professors and priests, while I searched for any upperclassman associated with a student paper or student government. But my ears and eyes lit on a shortish, grey-haired man with a great laugh, a loud voice and the darkest Italian tan I had ever seen.

He was holding court in the center of the student union building, such as it was, a 1960s multifunctional brick building that also housed the music room and the campus maintenance facility. I walked up to him, asked his name and what I should study in college. He told me I was now a student of the humanities and he would be my advisor. For lack of a better subject I had indicated English as my major on the application.

I have never lacked self-confidence — except on the sporting field — so I walked up to the freshman English faculty advisor with my student registration sheet and informed him that he would no longer be guiding my studies. Then I walked back to

Contris, handed him my sheet and told him to please indicate which courses I should take.

By that afternoon I was scheduled for the first year of studies, and I had started the school's first newspaper in decades. Finding a publisher was relatively easy. A local weekly offered to loan us their space for construction after hours, and I obtained startup money from the student government, which received money from "student activity fees" charged at registration. The student population numbered about 400, with an average age of 27. Many were military and married with children — and serious as a heart attack about their studies, which often involved their military career advancement and pay. As the 11th child of 13, I had no problem conversing with professors and 20- or 30-somethings, but I was not prepared for academic competition.

The military may not attract or promote divergent thinkers — and I was as divergent as they came. A 17-year-old, Catholic punk with an attitude against authority, I regretted being so young that I missed the 1960s civil rights movement and the Berkeley Free Speech Movement. I started one on campus a couple years later, but that's another story.

I was approached on three occasions by Benedictine monks as to whether I might feel a calling to the priesthood. I was never sure what they saw in me, but I loved philosophy, politics and religion in that order — much more a man of theory than one of practice. Each I time I responded, "Except for poverty, celibacy and obedience, I would." In college I was largely poor and mostly celibate, but *obedience* was — and is — the hard one for me. Ten years later, I was a featured speaker at a reunion dinner. I told the crowd that I had been approached three times, and I aways answered the same way. Now I came back, "a married, public school teacher. Which means I am poor, largely celibate, and completely obedient." The priests fell off their chairs laughing.

I cannot answer why I am not president of the United States, except to say, I don't yet have the money or name recognition to run. Perhaps if you all purchase these essays, my name will be in the mix for 2028. As for college professor, I would need an honorary degree, like Joan Baez or Bob Dylan. But here is my first book, for your edification and enjoyment. Please tell your friends.

Domestic Essays

Flynn and Other Conspirators Ought to be Stripped of Citizenship

A decorated general and former national security advisor actively participated in an attempted coup of the federal government. Then he refused to condemn his own actions in sworn testimony before the House Jan. 6 Committee, pleading the Fifth not only to his legal liability, but also to his moral culpability, and he refused to affirm the country's "peaceful transfer of power." How could he ever lead anyone in combat again?

Michael Flynn, Roger Stone, Rudy Giuliani, Donald Trump and Mark Meadows ought all to be stripped of their citizenship rights and expelled from the United States of America, like the treasonous Philip Nolan in the fictional *The Man without a Country* by Edward Everett Hale. Their traitorous actions on and before Jan. 6, 2021 — and their continued assistance and compliance with Donald Trump's coup attempt — merit no less punishment. Obviously, the Constitution calls for their execution; however, these are more civilized times. But irrevocable consequences must follow such insurrectionist behaviors.

So ought to be the punishment for 147 members of Congress who refused to certify the 2020 election in the hope of subverting democracy in the United States. At minimum they should be expelled from Congress. Then perhaps Congress will be capable of actually addressing global warming, immigration, healthcare, gun control, homelessness and multiple other pressing issues.

Following the Civil War, Confederate soldiers and others were required to swear an oath to the Constitution of the United States — or receive a presidential pardon — to regain their voting rights. So ought to be the case for all mentioned above.

The modern era's easy disregard for the rule of law reminds one of the Gilded Era of U.S. history: when Republicans, once idealists, degenerated into a conspiracy of wealth and corruption during the American Industrial Revolution. It took a few decades of unopposed Republican power to happen, and a world war, a depression and a New Deal to set right the economic apple cart.

The Jan. 6 Committee did the Lord's work to educate Americans, stranded in news deserts and cynically manipulated by right-wing media, to give them sufficient information to at least stop voting against their own interest. Hopefully, the committee reinvigorated the population to become angry enough to reengage in national politics and preserve self-government in the United States.

Supreme Madness: The Taliban United States Supreme Court

The complete contempt for women's bodily autonomy expressed by the Supreme Court at the end of the 2022 term astonishes, although the decision was telegraphed by someone in the building earlier in the year. This is clearly no longer the Roberts court, nor even the Thomas court. Instead the court aspires to be a fundamentalist Christian theocratic regime imposing an extreme paternalism on the nation state. So I suggest a more apt moniker: "The Taliban Supreme Court."

It is time Democrats start labeling abominations effectively — the better to move the middle toward renewing liberties long since thought won and secured. Dating back to my days in middle school, I was always curious as to why women don't march on Washington, D.C., armed to the teeth with pistols, shotguns and AK-47s wearing T-shirts with the slogan, "My Second Amendment Rights Protect My Ninth Amendment Rights." Pink "pussy hats" just aren't intimidating enough, and lack the gravitas appropriate to the current rights emergency.

Needless to say, anyone who does not vote pro-choice at every level of government does not respect women, especially women who are so conditioned by the patriarchy that they do not respect themselves. I get spiritual women, and men who recognize infanticide when they see it. But antiabortion laws are impossible to enforce without tyranny.

Also, constitutional amendments are past due. As a high school debate student, I argued the relative merits of the Electoral

College. Eliminating this pointless process would be neither new, radical or a threat to our democracy. In fact, it would be a solid step toward renewing democracy nationwide. I would begin with an amendment to eliminate the Electoral College. Of course, the process established by the founders is intentionally unwieldy and requires two-thirds of each house of Congress and approval by the state legislatures of three-fourths of the states. The likelihood of this happening in any of our lifetimes is close to zero. The Equal Rights Amendment was first drafted in 1923, and it is still not in the Constitution, although a significant number of states have adopted similar text for their state constitutions.

A more practical approach, already adopted by fifteen states and the District of Columbia, is entitled: The National Popular Vote Interstate Compact, a state-by-state attempt to circumvent the need for a constitutional amendment. It would not end the Electoral College, but redirect how it must operate. The initiative is well explained by Russell Berman for *The Atlantic.* Reports Mr. Berman, "binds them [participating states] to award their presidential electors to whichever candidate wins the most votes nationwide, even if another contender captured the most in their state. The accord will take effect once enough states representing 270 electoral votes pass the bill through their legislatures. As of now, the backers are 74 electoral votes short of that magic number."[1]

---

[1] Russell Berman, "The Secret to Beating the Electoral College," *The Atlantic*, Dec. 9, 2020,
https://www.theatlantic.com/politics/archive/2020/12/electoral-college-biden-trump/617338/ Accessed 29 April 2023.

Ironically, this mimics years of state-by-state antiabortion legislation; where conservative state legislatures passed laws banning abortion retroactively (to various degrees) pending a Supreme Court reversal of Roe v Wade. Which, as one may have heard, happened at the end of the end of the 2021-22 Supreme Court session.

For those interested in a 'deep dive' on the issue (remember I debated this in high school — *1975*) I recommend downloading a Feb. 9, 2009 Congressional Service Report: *Electoral College Reform: 110th Congress Proposals, the National Popular Vote Campaign, and Other Alternative Developments.*[2]

A second constitutional amendment is necessary to end gerrymandering. Every state should have a diverse citizens' commission aided by statisticians, computer programs and sociologists. Passing the John Lewis Voting Rights Advancement Act is a necessary hedge against institutional racism and dishonest politics.

The outrage of Citizens United may also require an amendment, in order to level the election playing field and deter self-financed and purchased candidates.

Citizens' United is legal shorthand for a seven-page majority Supreme Court decision which held that 'money equals speech, a principle first established 800 B.C. according to Wikipedia, "India, as early as 800 BC, granted legal personhood to guild-like *śreṇī* that operated in the public interest. The late Roman

---

[2] https://crsreports.congress.gov/product/pdf/RL/RL34604/7. Accessed 29 April 2023.

Republic granted legal personhood to municipalities, public works companies that managed public services, and voluntary associations (*collegia*) such as the early Catholic Church."

The arguments against this absurdist thinking are myriad throughout history. Please imagine a corporation named SHYLOCK.COM. "If you cut us, do we not bleed? Oh, that's right, we don't!" My favorite objection was a picket sign reading, "I'll believe corporations are people when *Texas executes one.*"

There is also a case to be made for mandatory retirement ages for the judiciary. Justice Ginsberg did us no favors by not retiring in the first two years of the Obama administration, when a suitable liberal would have been easily confirmed.

Another step toward protecting rights would be ending the filibuster in the U.S. Senate, or at least returning to the old rules of the "standing" filibuster. The practice of sending an anonymous note to the Senate Majority Leader, protesting any action on any subject, is the most antidemocratic practice of the most antidemocratic half of the U.S. federal government.

Finally, true gender equity will only arrive when governments at all levels adopt a practice common to the Democratic Party back when I was a district chair. The rule was simple: If the chair elected was male, the vice-chair could only be a woman, and vice versa, through all remaining positions, treasurer, sergeant at arms, etc. Michele Swers, of Georgetown University, wrote a well-documented work on this subject, *The Difference Women*

Make: The Policy Impact of Women in Congress, that I just added to my must-read list.

Obviously, the recommendations above may take a lifetime of civic engagement, but I am recently retired and ready to roll up my sleeves. Many political innovations begin at the local level before becoming national movements. The $15 minimum wage began as a union pipe dream in Tukwila, Washington, before catching on nationally. The 17th Amendment — allowing direct elections of senators by the people — is another example.

Nothing in a democracy is impossible. It just takes faith and commitment to the process, which is in itself a commitment to the community. At age 18, all the men and women of Athens were administered the "Athenian Oath." One translation includes, "We will fight for the ideals and sacred things of the city, both alone and with many." So the future starts now, citizens.

The Roman Catholic Church's Pagan Birth Control and Abortion Dogma

Section V, paragraph 1643 of the *Catechism of the Catholic Church* states: "[Marriage] aims at a deeply personal unity, a unity that, beyond union in one flesh, leads to forming one's heart and soul; it demands *indissolubility* (italics theirs) and *faithfulness* (ditto) in definitive mutual giving; and is open to *fertility* (again ditto)."

— Libreria Editrice Vaticana, 1992 edition

So how did this dogma become the theology driving the recent U.S. Supreme Court nullification of Roe v. Wade, and the violation of every American woman's bodily autonomy? Simple. It began with a pagan philosopher named Aristotle, whose attempts at rudimentary natural philosophy theorized four causes of existence.

Formally stated they are: the formal cause, the actual shape of a physical entity; the material cause, human flesh; the efficient cause, sexual intercourse; and the final cause, a teleological idea that presumes every aspect of the universe has a perceivable *purpose* (italics mine). This last aspect of the theory has haunted Western civilization to this day. Aristotle was lost to Western Europe with the fall of Rome, but rediscovered with the fall of Toledo, Spain, and the subsequent transfer of dozens of the world's best libraries from Islamic control to Catholic control in the middle of the 13th century. This also sparked the European Renaissance..

From 1268 to 1274 Saint Thomas Aquinas composed *On the Soul,* fully integrating the *natural philosophy* of the recently rediscovered Aristotle into (then) contemporary Catholic teaching. Sadly, this misguided Aristotelian hunch has never been fully excised from Catholic dogma, and wasn't ejected from science until the 20th century. *On the Origin of Species* by Darwin perpetuates Aristotelian "final cause" notions, regarding Nature as a self-determining collective of living entities. This philosophy theorizes that evolutionary forces are working toward "perfection," a notion clearly evident in subtext and premise of Darwin's classic work.

Needless to say, modern evolutionary biologists have recognized this early error and substituted *random mutation* and *natural selection* in its place. Darwin began using these concepts, but the echo of Aristotle remains in his work for those readers attuned to the sound. I was surprised to hear Aristotle clearly on my first reading of *Origin of Species*.

Supreme Court Justices Alito (who wrote the majority opinion reversing Roe), Thomas (who wrote a concurring opinion), Sotomayor, Gorsuch, Roberts, Kavanaugh and Barrett are all Catholic (Gorsuch converted to the near equivalent Episcopalian). Kagan is the only justice of Jewish faith (Stephen Breyer retired in the fall of 2022). Sotomayor joining Kagan and Breyer in dissent demonstrates that not all religious and legal scholars are of the same mind.

Interestingly, Kagan's Jewish faith inspires her vehement dissent, as Judaism does not consider life to begin until the first breath of the child.

The Supreme Court has long been dominated by jurors of religious traditions noted for theological and philosophical scholarship. It is an obvious advantage when interpreting laws and constitutions — which inherently have a *final cause* component. Reread the Preamble to the U.S. Constitution, and appreciate how strongly *final cause* intentionality resonates:
". . . in Order to form a more perfect Union, establish Justice, insure domestic Tranquility, provide for the common defense, promote the general Welfare . . ."

As a practicing Catholic, I apologize to the women of the United States for the undue influence my religion has on current political reality, and am ashamed that my church has not faced its most egregious error of reasoning, which has been readily apparent to anyone with an education since the Renaissance.

Open Letter to Justice Clarence Thomas: One Catholic to Another

Brother in the Risen Christ:

One can only imagine your current sadness and suffering resulting from the reaction to your concurring opinion with Justice Alito's reversal of Roe v. Wade. Speculation about what the new "conservative majority" might impose on the United States citizenry includes angst regarding birth control, homosexual marriage, and affirmative action. Doubtless, countless curses and invectives against your well-being are hurled at you daily. I know I have heard an astounding number of them myself.

You are falsely accused of pursuing a purely political agenda, when all who like myself have studied your opinions, know that you pursue God's justice on earth, legislating good works as legal imperatives to save the souls of the helpless, anchoring the U.S. legal system in truth, and improving the virtue of citizens regardless of race, sex or religious affiliation.

That you would eventually rule to overturn Roe — when given an opportunity — was entirely self-evident to anyone who bothered to take your faith and your testimony in the confirmation hearings seriously.

Blatant evidence screamed out in the third point of your Obergefell v. Hodges dissent. As you know, Obergefell's majority decision, authored by Justice Anthony Kennedy, mischaracterized the source of human dignity severely —

literally standing the moral concept on its head in order to justify judicial social engineering of law, so as to better reflect emerging cultural tolerance, and acceptance of homosexual relationships as families.

The story of Western civilization has been one of slow progress toward recognizing the innate human dignity of all human beings and their right to "life, liberty and the pursuit of happiness." As that dignity comes from "their Creator," it is not possible for governments to bestow dignity on any individual or group within its borders, or to deny it. You wisely opined:

> *The corollary of that principle is that human dignity cannot be taken away by the government. Slaves did not lose their dignity (any more than they lost their humanity) because the government allowed them to be enslaved. Those held in internment camps did not lose their dignity because the government confined them. And those denied governmental benefits certainly do not lose their dignity because the government denies them those benefits. The government cannot bestow dignity, and it cannot take it away.*

Recently, you have been roundly criticized by the political class for simply expounding on the obvious implications of this universal truth when applied to law and previous court decisions. Unique life begins in a woman's womb at fertilization, and possesses full human dignity from that moment on. It is every woman's blessing to nurture each human individual with which she is gifted, through its birth and childhood. It is a man's responsibility to lend all aid and support in this endeavor, provide for, protect and model responsible male behavior.

Failure to do so by either party is sin — moving oneself away from God's grace — and failing to realize one's best self. You indicated as much at your hearings, identifying yourself as a practicing Roman Catholic, and testifying to your efforts to promote affirmative action at the federal level. Affirmative action is, of course, moral government policy to promote the acceptance of all human dignity through employment law, education law, investment law, housing law, and countless other government interventions to promote virtuous behavior in the United States.

Your answers to various senators regarding whether women have a right to privacy protecting abortion rights are so obviously a mealy-mouthed, intellectual dodge, it is astounding any Senate Democrat voted to confirm without a guarantee from you to protect Roe. Did they seriously think you would be objective, given your faith, work history and testimony? Brother, it is not you who have betrayed American women; it was the willful blindness of the confirmation committee. One speculates that they were so eager to get an African American back on the court, that they seem to have forgotten that the Republican Party platform calls outright for the reversal of Roe. And has done so since 1980.

I feel sorry for your current suffering, but I know you work to realize God's will to the best of your judgment. I have but one question and concern regarding future cases you choose to hear and decisions you may reverse.

You have mentioned reconsidering Griswold v. Connecticut, the decision upholding a woman's right to privacy and birth control in consultation with her medical professional. But Americans may not comprehend why you perceive the decision so egregious. It was, of course, Saint Thomas Aquinas' cribbing of Aristotle's final cause theory that is the true origin of Catholic dogma regarding the sin of birth control.

Final cause, as we both know, was Aristotle's idea that everything, including human activity has a teleological end intended by nature. Failure to allow the entity to fulfill its destiny was to interfere with natural law itself. Aquinas instantly recognized the pagan was onto something, but that Aristotle was ignorant of the One True God; or he would have surmised the full implications of the theory, and its obvious relevance to the human reproductive act. Obviously, contraception foils the final cause of sexual intercourse, mostly preventing sperm from fertilizing egg, and preventing the realization of God's will for every man and woman.

Many Americans will likely be shocked that their current liberties are in danger of being reversed by a Supreme Court Justice's application of an ancient Greek scientific theory, adapted by a Catholic saint and scholar, and likely to be applied sooner rather than later to contraceptive law in the United States of America.

Brother Thomas, I implore you to pray long and hard about this issue. The moral justification for reversal is obvious to us. However, one of the joys of freedom in the United States is tolerance for other religions, lifestyles, values, and morals. I am unclear how this could possibly be preserved in the future, in light of a reversal of Griswold and other contraception laws. Obviously, it would be desirable if all men and women choose to willingly follow God's and the church's moral teaching. The only way to enforce such a ban would require intolerable monitoring of adult sexuality, and a dystopian form of coercion imagined by Margaret Atwood in *The Handmaid's Tale.* Finally, please remember, contraception is the best way to realistically prevent abortions.

Again, please pray hard on this, and be sure you follow God's will, and that personal pride or hubris does not blind your judgment.

Yours in the Risen Christ,

James Matthew Sawatzki

Solving Homelessness in One Easy Step

Finland boasts a national homeless housing agency that has all but eliminated homelessness throughout the country. It is called The Housing Finance and Development Centre of Finland. Its policy is tried and true: Housing first, housing immediately, no questions asked, no immediate requirements, no need to pass Go, no need to deposit $200, no Puritanical judgments about lifestyle, no need to be a citizen of Finland.

The United States lives in mortal sin from its neglect of the homeless. A 2020 estimate of the number of our fellow citizens homeless each evening is 580,466 — far too many of them children also experiencing food insecurity and lack of medical care..[3] An appalling number given this nation's status as the wealthiest in human history.

The United Nations considers housing a human right; a document on the matter by the U.N. states, "Homelessness is the unacceptable result of States failing to implement the right to adequate housing. It requires urgent and immediate human rights responses by the international community and by all States."[4]

---

[3] Stasha, S. (2022, September 29). The State Of Homelessness In The US — 2022. *Policy Advice*. Policyadvice.net. Retrieved December 3, 2022, from https://policyadvice.net/contact-us/.

[4] United Nations. (2016, February 26). A/HRC/34/51: Report of the special rapporteur on adequate housing as a component of the right to an adequate standard of living, and on the right to non-discrimination in this context. OHCHR. Retrieved July 8, 2022, from https://www.ohchr.org/en/documents/thematic-reports/ahrc3451-report-special-rapporteur-adequate-housing-component-right.

The U.N. passed the first international resolution on homelessness. In presenting the resolution on its website, the agency quotes Chris Gardner, author of *The Pursuit of Happyness:* "It could happen to anyone. It's not always drugs, alcohol. Life happens. And life can happen to a whole lot of us. It did during the great financial crisis, and it could very well happen again."[5]

Efforts to house homeless veterans by the U.S. Department of Veterans Affairs and non-governmental organizations, such as Homes for Our Troops, have made heroic progress in the last several years, meeting 81% of the VA's goal. These efforts, focused on a single population, serve as a model for what local, state and other federal departments ought to be doing yesterday.[6]

Currently, the only U.S. federal agency dealing wholly with homelessness is the U.S. Interagency Council on Homelessness (USICH). It is committed to racial equality, housing first, and decriminalization of homelessness. In ten years its efforts have reduced homelessness 9% nationwide, but have achieved 30% to 50% reduction in veteran homelessness. The USICH website

---

[5] United Nations: Department of Economic and Social Affairs. (2020, March 9). *First-ever United Nations resolution on homelessness | DISD*. First Ever United Nations Resolution on Homelessness. Retrieved July 8, 2022, from https://www.un.org/development/desa/dspd/2020/03/resolution-homelessness/.

[6] Weis-Corbley, G. (Ed.). (2022, November 17). *U.S. near its goal to house every homeless veteran identified in a January 2022 count*. Good News Network. Retrieved July 8, 2022, from https://www.goodnewsnetwork.org/us-meeting-2022-goal-of-housing-every-homeless-veteran/.

contains links to a state-by-state accounting of homeless populations, and a list of tested tools and procedures for addressing homelessness at the neighborhood and local levels.[7]

So what are we waiting for?

---

[7] U.S. Interagency Council on Homelessness, https://www.usich.gov/

Overhauling College Education Programs toward Effectiveness: A Modest Proposal of Educational Reform

In its most pure form, education is primarily about storytelling. I could stop here, because everything about to be recommended is a logical consequence of this fact, but that would require the reader to have equivalent experience in education to myself — which is unlikely — so I will continue.

College education programs are so ill-equipped, and so misguided about the nature of learning, that they are essentially — on the whole — worthless, functioning only to pad the university's bottom line, and to perpetuate the education departments themselves. Moreover, their general incompetence more often does more harm than good to teacher formation, which further harms the effectiveness of public education and disadvantages children.

Education is everything in the modern world. Education is a living wage; education is citizenship; education is upward mobility; education is international mobility. Education is where you live. Education is where your offspring go to school. Education is whether your child will die at an early age from gun violence. The stakes are high.

The stakes are so high that colleges and universities cannot morally charge the outrageous sums they do to deliver a failed skill set. I could make a case for training teachers the way electricians learn, as journeymen en route to receiving their union license. However, that would probably only work for elementary and perhaps middle school teachers. High school teachers actually need specialized expertise in college curricula. All sorts of expertise — like sciences, history, literature and algebra — so that they can model scholastic discipline for students. This kind of specialized knowledge is best obtained in higher learning.

Primarily, teachers have to know how to tell a story, effectively and in many different ways, in order to connect with every individual and learning style in the classroom. This takes practice, training and imagination. And the vast majority of public school teachers lack these skills.

Years ago, I advocated that colleges of education should be transferred en masse to the relevant theater department at each college and university. Quality teaching resembles troupe improvisation far more than it resembles scholarship, military training, or academics. The reason is simple.

Students must become active participants in the storytelling, shaping their own stories, abilities, experiences, and skills as they play out their own imagined future selves; becoming the best possible selves their inclinations and desires crave.

As handmaidens to this transformation, teachers must match relevant state requirements to individual student goals, while promoting mastery of academic skills requisite for success in life and college.

Interpersonal communication skills are the top requirement for teachers today and tomorrow. Mastering a particular lesson plan can happen the night before the lesson, but communicating effectively with 35 diverse individuals — that skill takes talent, practice, knowledge, and experience.

Equally important is effective parent communication. The number of teachers who are petrified of calling home to chat with a parent — with positive or negative news — astounds. Most teachers today do not even want their home phone numbers to be public. They further demand that any expectation by the school district to contact parents be financially compensated during working hours, as though they are day laborers punching a clock. This is what public education has become.

It was not always so. In the 1960s public education in California was generously funded and the California system of colleges — including the innovation of community college — made it the leading state in the nation producing college graduates and professionals. It also stimulated the housing market, sparking a bonanza of new arrivals from national and international locales.

This further sparked a boom in education programs — a fine middle-class profession — and the need for more teachers during the resulting baby boom. Unfortunately, it also created a burdensome bureaucracy, and the requisite regulations and paperwork required to perpetuate said bureaucracy. Students fell through cracks in the regulations, and restrictions on academic freedom began.

Progressive states across the nation followed California's lead, resulting in the public education landscape we have today. Unfortunately, that IS the problem.

After about five years of teaching experience, 1984–89, I realized that what public education needed, more than anything else, was *perestroika*. The public school choice campaign was ascendant at the time, and parents were demanding alternative options for their children. Many did so because they were privileged but did not want to pay for private school; others were motivated by social justice and the disproportionate quality of public schools between suburbs and inner cities.

I was particularly motivated by a conversation with a Baptist minister in South Seattle, regarding how unresponsive he found Seattle Public Schools to the needs of his parishioners.

The same week an article appeared in the local newspaper regarding the efforts of a Seattle couple to bring school choice to the state of Washington. They were motivated by progressive intentions, recognizing their own privilege to send their children to elite private schools, while fellow citizens languished in Seattle's pedestrian public schools. They thought innovation might be the solution; after all, it was the early Clinton era, and hope was in the air.

My union, the Washington Education Association, was less than impressed. I was on the communication subcommittee. Our only real job was to choose the WEA Teacher of the Year from the several applicants — always fewer than six.

The Seattle couple — a pair of lawyers — wrote a unique bill to alter the licensing of public educators. The bill proposed giving teachers the same status in law as doctors and lawyers, such that only licensed teachers could authorize more teachers, the way that only licensed doctors and lawyers can authorize members of their professions. Teachers would, once again, become members of a privileged guild, limiting the number of practitioners so as to guarantee a particular level of income. A free market solution borrowed from the Middle Ages and applied to the global economy.

Moreover, it would guarantee licensed teachers' absolute authority over educational practices, standards of academic achievement and promotion of students through the various grades and on to higher education. It was complete professional empowerment for each teacher — and the Washington Education Association freaked out!

I communicated to the chair of the WEA (early internet) that I would contact this couple and arrange a meeting between them and the WEA Board of Directors at the next meeting. I was instructed and encouraged to do so.

Then I began a summer-long email exchange with the couple, even visiting them, at their summer home in Snoqualmie, Washington.

Imagine my astonishment, when at the start of the meeting, I was instructed by the chair to "shut up and sit down," when I began introductions at the start of the meeting.

What followed was an inquisition not witnessed since the McCarthy era. The WEA board was loaded for bear with detailed intelligence of all the couple's movements over the summer: which cities they visited, which conferences they attended, which education reform organizations they held meetings with, which donors to private school choice they solicited. Most egregiously, they had attended a California conference promoting parental school choice for religious schools.

As a Catholic school student myself — first grade through college — and a former Teamster, I knew the couple's dreams for Seattle's students, and my hope of educational reform, were doomed by the individuals in this room. They would not hear of alternate options, ever. Their most common statements referenced segregated schools in the South, during their youth. Never mind the actual fact that schools are as segregated in Seattle today as they were in the 1950s.

My other favorite school choice fact is that 36% of Seattle public school teachers send their own children to private religious schools. But of course, with union wages, they can afford to do so.

My most vivid memory of the next WEA convention in Bellevue, Washington late that summer, was the sight of 2,200 delegates from throughout Washington state voting to refuse to hear my legislative proposal to the convention. Thanks to the intervention of the parliamentarian, I was allowed to speak by a technicality. According to Robert's Rules of Order, one cannot defeat a motion before it is proposed.

The other most vivid memory is attending the WEA Republican Delegates Caucus that weekend. It was held in a hotel room. Eight delegates were present. They listened to my proposal patiently, then voted that far more pressing and realistic issues needed to be addressed. Complete lack of imagination and foresight by educational professionals is why progress does not occur in public education.

The other 2,012-ish delegates met at the Democratic Caucus in the convention center main hall to endorse approved candidates for state and federal public office. Every vote a voice vote. Every vote unanimous. No dissension from the floor against common consensus. It might as well have been the Politburo.

Just Open the Borders – Let All Who Wish to be Americans in, Without Limits

A quick Google search for "immigration reports" reveals sixteen separate reports and studies supporting open borders to the United States — on the first page. Immigrants of all kinds, documented and undocumented, are on balance, such a positive economic and cultural benefit to the U.S. that maintaining current, ineffective, immoral anti-immigration policies is irrational.

The reports range from the ultra-Libertarian Cato Institute, to the White House Immigration website of the Biden administration, to the National Academies of Sciences, Engineering and Medicine, to the Carnegie Corporation and the Migration Policy Institute. Each report advocates for less restrictive laws, rules, and regulations regarding immigration.

Immigrants create jobs

On average, immigrants start more small businesses than second generation Americans. "In the United States, where 13.7% of the population is foreign-born, immigrants represent 20.2% of the self-employed workforce and 25% of startup founders."[8]

---

[8] "Immigration, Upward Mobility, and the U.S. Economy," *Harvard Business Review*, HBR IdeaCast, Episode 860
https://hbr.org/podcast/2022/05/immigration-upward-mobility-and-the-u-s-economy.

Immigrants are not a drain on social services

The U.S. Center on Budget and Policy Priorities stated:

> *We find that the large majority of those who ever used benefits were also employed a majority of the time, and even more were either employed or had an employed spouse:*
>
> - *At least 93 percent were either employed in the majority of the observed years (five or more of the nine years observed in our PSID sample) or were married to someone who was.*
> - *77 percent of such immigrant program participants were themselves employed in a majority of the observed years.*
> - *At least 87 percent were either employed themselves at the time of the final interview in 2015 or were married to someone who was.*[9]

Immigrants produce less crime

"Immigrants, including illegal immigrants, are less likely to be incarcerated in prisons, convicted of crimes, or arrested than native-born Americans."[10]

---

[9] Arloc Sherman, Danilo Trisi, Chad Stone, Shelby Gonzales and Sharon Parrott, "Immigrants Contribute Greatly to U.S. Economy, Despite Administration's "Public Charge" Rule Rationale," Center on Budget and Policy Priorities, published Aug. 15, 2019, accessed Aug. 30, 2022, https://www.cbpp.org/research/poverty-and-inequality/immigrants-contribute-greatly-to-us-economy-despite-administrations.

[10] "15 Myths About Immigration Debunked," Carnegie Corporation of New York, Sept. 27, 2021, accessed April 29, 2023, https://www.carnegie.org/our-work/article/15-myths-about-immigration-debunked/.

Immigrants support the agricultural industry: Bracero Program

The Bracero Program was a 1942 immigration policy to replace the tens of thousands of agricultural workers absorbed by the war effort, by actively recruiting Mexican citizens living near the border to migrate during harvest seasons in the United States. By the time the program officially ended in 1964, immigration workers had become integral to U.S. agricultural industries. Seasonal migration continues to this day with legal and undocumented workers, without whom crops could not be harvested in a timely manner.

"With a growing population, immigrant labor is vital to helping the agriculture industry produce the food required to feed Americans. By 2050, 9.6 billion people will be living on our planet, with over 400 million people living in the United States, making it the fourth most populous country in the world."[11] So concludes multiple studies by Americas Society and Council of the Americas.

Open borders have proven wildly effective in the European Union

The National Bureau of Economic Research reports:
> *In Kennan (2013) it was shown that the potential gains from open borders are very large: if all of the developed countries dropped all legal restrictions on*

---

[11] "Get the Facts: Five Reasons Why Immigrants Are Critical for Our Agricultural Sector," Americas Society/Council of the Americas, published Aug. 28, 2013, accessed April 29, 2023, https://www.as-coa.org/articles/get-facts-five-reasons-why-immigrants-are-critical-our-agricultural-sector.

immigration, the gains would be roughly comparable to a doubling of the income of the average person in a less developed country. The European Union has actually implemented an open borders regime, and the expansion of the EU to include many large countries with relatively low wages provides some evidence on the extent to which these gains are actually realized.[12]

Who doesn't want immigration? Republican fearmongers, racists and Cubans in Florida

Besides former President "Shithole Countries" Trump and similar "America Firsters," few who have studied immigration oppose relaxed U.S. immigration laws, except racists, and a politically powerful minority in Florida — Cuban Americans. Cuban Americans lobby both major political parties relentlessly to maintain economic pressure on their former homeland. They hold a strong grudge against Cuba's communist government, and resent being prevented by Cuba from receiving compensation for properties they left behind in the Cuban Revolution. Doubtless many supported the dictator Fulgencio Batista, and deserved being dispossessed.

Today, U.S. relations with Latin America are suffering from an equally irrational policy toward Cuba — a policy designed in the 1960s to overthrow Fidel Castro's government and which, more than 50 years later, is no closer to success. Like U.S. policy toward

---

[12] John Kennan, "Open Borders in the European Union and Beyond: Migration Flows and Labor Market Implications," National Bureau of Economic Research, Jan 2017, accessed April 29, 2023, https://www.nber.org/papers/w23048.

China in the 1950s and 1960s, policy toward Cuba is frozen in place by a domestic political lobby, this one with roots in the electorally pivotal state of Florida.[13]

President Obama relaxed sanctions a bit, allowing for "educational" tourism, but Congress has refused to change the sanctions, so with the Trump administration, boycotts snapped back into place. This despite the fact that the U.S. has established and mutually lucrative trade treaties with both Vietnam and The People's Republic of China.

For decades, an education colleague of mine regularly quipped, "Sawatzki, you continue to make the same error in reasoning. You are attempting to use logic in an inherently illogical situation." It will remain so, until citizens put reason back in charge for U.S. international policies.

---

[13] William M. LeoGrande, "The Cuba Lobby," *Foreign Policy*, (April 12, 2013), accessed Aug. 30, 2022, https://foreignpolicy.com/2013/04/12/the-cuba-lobby/.

Foreign Policy Essays

Solving the Israeli – Palestinian Crisis

Never has a simple three-paragraph memo caused more bloodshed and conflict than the 1917 Balfour Declaration by the British Government, which tried to encourage Zionism in Palestine while simultaneously avoiding harm to Palestinian citizenship rights. Talk about unintentional blunders in foreign policy by imperialists ignorant of facts on the ground.

Following the end of the British Mandate, the newly formed United Nations proposed a "two-state" partition of Palestine to end decades of conflict. No fewer than eight U.N. resolutions and declarations have since followed — the most recent, Resolution 2334 in 2014 — reinforces the original partition and calls on all parties to negotiate borders and processes. Both sides have been recalcitrant, walking away from negotiations dozens of times.

Further, both sides hold unreasonable and unrealistic demands, including claiming Jerusalem for their national capitals. Israel is especially obstinate in refusing to share Jerusalem. The solution to this deadlock is simple, but requires politicians stand up to the Jewish international lobbying efforts, and their own Jewish constituents, who are always ready to "wave the bloody shirt of the Holocaust" to foil attempts to pressure Israel to compromise.

A resolution to the standoff is simply achieved. The United States, Iran, Saudi Arabia, Egypt and Turkey need coordinated diplomacy, exercising a simple "carrot and stick" foreign policy to drive both parties back to the negotiating table, with economic incentives and international penalties for resolving the problem. According to the BBC the U.S. gifted Israel $38 billion — mostly military aid — in 2016 and $3.8 billion in 2020. International aid to Palestine averages about $757 million a year.[14]

The conditions both sides need to be forced to accept are four:

- Jerusalem will become the first "U.N. International City" where all are welcome and it will not function as a national capital for any nation. (The U.S. must remove its embassy.)
- Israel will be forced to pay reparations for decades of moral and economic exploitation of the Palestinian people. Every adult Palestinian shall receive appropriate restitution for lost properties, opportunities and pain and suffering.
- These immediate penalties will be accompanied by international economic and investment incentives for both Israel and Palestine.
- To pay for this, the nations involved will be encouraged to adopt a "yearly wealth" tax on their billionaire citizens. Heck, Elon Musk could fund the entire enterprise himself as a charitable donation, and for a statue of him in the holiest part of Jerusalem.

Only resolve is needed by the international community of nations to end the suffering of the Palestinian people once and

---

[14] Jake Horton, "Israel-Gaza: How much money does Israel get from the US?," BBC News, May 24, 2021, accessed April 29, 2023, https://www.bbc.com/news/57170576.

for all time. Both nations' economies will explode with growth from new investments, manufacturing, tourism, finance, and commerce. Quality of life for all will improve, and hopefully, eventually, both nations will come to respect each other and cooperate while working to maintain peace in the Middle East.

Fixing Ineffective US and UN Foreign Policies in the Middle East

An outsized political minority with undue influence in Congress comprises those of Jewish ancestry or faith. People from all sects of Judaism exert political influence, as do members of all Christian sects. (Followers of Islam are not a large enough presence in the states to have any significant influence, despite Christian fundamentalist rhetoric.) And it is appropriate that they engage in lawmaking, to promote their values and goals for the American experiment.

On whole, religious influence in U.S. law making has been a net benefit. The abolitionist movement to end slavery began in liberal-leaning Christian congregations. The U.S. labor movement benefited from ecumenical support throughout the decades. Modern civil rights leaders have marched alongside religious leaders of all varieties, and the 1950s and '60s voting rights movement organized in Baptist churches.

Social justice movements continue to motivate religious organizations to: abolish the death penalty; end homelessness, protect social safety nets, end race prejudice, prevent nuclear war, reform church leaderships, empower women as religious leaders, feed the world, and prevent global warming, just to name a few.

Unfortunately, too many moderate and conservative practitioners of Judaism militantly support robust economic military and economic aid to Israel — in violation of long-standing foreign policy — and against the U.S.'s own political interests.

One can hardly blame Israel, following the Holocaust, centuries of second-class citizenship in Europe, the diaspora, and oppression from the Roman Empire, even after being released from Babylon, and their mythohistorical enslavement in Egypt.

However, their history of oppression does not justify the perpetual oppression of Palestinians, victims of the creation of the State of Israel, and several subsequent wars to preserve that unjust state against Arab invasions. The U.S. is particularly responsible for the situation, as it was the first nation to recognize Israel's independence, and as author of the modern United Nations, which maintains the world's political stasis and entrenched injustices.

The solution is obvious, and has been known to all since before the state of Israel's founding. It was originally proposed before Israel was recognized, but at the time, fundamentally unenforceable. That is no longer the case. The U.N. needs to declare Jerusalem an "International City" or "International Heritage Site" and administer the city as a protectorate for all of humanity.

This only requires a willingness to do so. Sure, Israel is capable of resisting occupation, and creating civil unrest, as it did in its creation — but after being deprived of economic and military support for a couple years, and faced with the combined military might of the United Nations, I suspect they will acquiesce, rather than see Jerusalem leveled for the third time in its history.

Obviously, this does not end potential conflict between Jews and Muslims within the city going into the future, but with international police maintaining the peace, perhaps intifadas and firing on Arab civilians will end. It will also need to end all continuing settlements in the West Bank, open access to the Gaza Strip, and generally allow free-flowing economic development in both. This will empower Arabs in Israel and raised them out of poverty, turning multigenerational refugee camps into thriving cities.

This compromise allows both faiths to possess Jerusalem as their capital, while a neutral third party governs the city. An alternative is requiring Israel to return to Tel Aviv for its capital, denying the label of government capital to both Jews and Muslims.

Ending the Islamic faith schism of A.D. 632 — also helpful

The second U.N. and U.S. intervention needed to stabilize the Middle East is to negotiate a conclusion to the Islamic faith's schism of A.D. 632. Since the death of Mohammed, Sunni and Shia Muslims have battled over hierarchical authority. This is the kind of juvenile nonsense one expects from the Roman Catholic Church of the Middle Ages.

It serves as "cover" excusing the corrupt political motivations of Saudi Arabia, Iraq, Iran and Afghanistan, as well as other minor players in the political psychodrama. The solution is simple, a complete divorce. The faith already has brokered a kind of cooperative separation, allowing Muslims of all faiths to make Hajj.

Obviously, economic pressure and military threats will be necessary from Western nations, to prevent violent activities between Middle Eastern nation-states plotting actions to promote their own economic and military interest against each other. Actual territorial grabs of acreage from other nation-states, as in the first Iraq War, must be prevented, but that should not be too burdensome with the current global economy.

Ending sanctions on Iran, and allowing (perhaps encouraging) the country to build nuclear resources, may well stabilize the region. Its leaders are not fanatical terrorists, but they will use terrorism as part of asymmetrical warfare to counter latent colonial powers and interests.

India, Pakistan, and Israel each have a nuclear arsenal. There is no reason Iran should not develop peaceful nuclear technology. It may in fact promote stability, improve discourse and possibly promote trade and economic ties among all nations in this troubled region.

The Powerless: Of Witch Hunts, Red Scares, Richard Hofstadter, UFOs and Marjorie Taylor Greene

The January/February 2023 issue of *The Atlantic* featured a motivational analysis of Georgia U.S. Representative Marjorie Taylor Greene by Elaina Plott Calabro.[15] An excellent profile resulting from thorough research, personal interviews with those who knew her from school days, through marriage, and more than one career, before she found her calling — exposing the hidden international powers which collude to undermine democracy, morality, and capitalism in every nation on earth.

Ms. Plott Calabro strings together facts of the representative's youth, experience and disappointments, providing a credible personality profile providing insight to Ms. Greene's embrace of paranoid conspiracy theories, contempt for rule of law, and "culture warrior" political persona. The article also reveals how desperate the representative is for public attention, affirmation, and a sense of personal identity. It is this desperation to find "meaning" in her life that clearly motivates her most extreme behaviors, and total disregard for propriety, due process, facts, and evidence. Taylor Greene makes no distinction between personal perception and objective truth, a failing of rational thought all too common in the United States, and far too many other nations, today.

---

[15] Elaina Plott Calabro, "Why Is Marjorie Taylor Greene Like This?," *The Atlantic*, January/February 2023, https://www.theatlantic.com/magazine/archive/2023/01/marjorie-taylor-greene-congress-georgia-election-background/672229/.

Of course, this is by no means the first or last time the U.S. or other nations have fomented political movements or religious cults promising redemption through "secret knowledge" and membership in a revolutionary crusade against shadowy, entrenched oppressive powers. The converted are convinced that "sheeple" do not recognize those who control international economics, international law, and the entire public and private education system – especially higher education such as college and post-graduate studies.

The list of anti-intellectual movements motivating rebellion against perceived bastions of power, and far too often, spilling over into actual violence in the United States is long, curious, and varied. It reflects an undying paranoia latent within U.S. culture, and all cultures where a significant segment of the population feels powerless, unheard, unrepresented, and that their personal values and identify are threatened by they know not what.

These public fever dreams date back to our earliest settlers, fearful of the forest and the native tribes living in them: the Salem Witch Trials, anti-federalist sentiment in colonial and early U.S. history, the Civil War, the Ku Klux Klan, the Chinese Exclusion Act, the First and Second Red Scares, White Citizens' Councils and Jim Crow era segregation laws, "The Protocols of the Elders of Zion," the John Birch Society, Ayn Rand and her minions, UFOs, the Trilateral Commission, end-of-the-world cults such as Jonestown, and the most recent outbreak — The Q-anon Conspiracy Theory and backlash against Critical Race Theory. Not to mention, a stubborn strain of racism and fascism that resides — at least in part – in the minds of too many U.S.

citizens. A brief introduction to each of the references in this paragraph will be at the end of this chapter.

Richard Hofstadter's brilliant analysis, "The Paranoid Style in American Politics," published in *Harper's Magazine* in Nov. 1964, is a must-read for all who wish to comprehend the source of U.S. mass delusions, fears, and conspiracy theories. Paired with George Orwell's classic essay, *Politics and the English Language,* the two form an excellent primer on conspiracy-based political movements and how certain politicians exploit these manias for personal political power. They are at least as important reading as Machiavelli's *The Prince* as an introduction to political science and the art of ruling what Aristotle labeled "a warlike hoard," his term for the average citizenry in a democracy. (All three works are available as PDFs for free on the Internet.)

Multiple psychological and sociological studies have demonstrated that the human mind is a meaning making machine, and presented with a random array of facts and interrelationships, will superimpose on the data a personally generated pattern of association that reveals a cause or a course of the random data. Humans can't stop this from happening. They can, however, be aware of this interpretive tendency in themselves and others, and hold suspect even their own analysis of what they experience. This is, of course, the first step in the scientific method.

However, a sense of powerlessness over one's personal life is fertile ground for indoctrination by other paranoid minds to share a "special knowledge" explaining what goes on behind the curtain among individuals and institutions that are perceived to be more powerful or entitled than oneself. Fear of a lack of access, followed by a fear of a lack of insider information, threatens the individual's sense of equality and participation. This results in resentment against the system and the individuals they perceive manipulate control it.

Such an alienated mind soon comes to project conspiratorial relationships between all the systems of the "ruling classes," such that open resistance to legal structures is seen as the only possible reaction to their own collective sense of being exploited. Motivated by a sense of righteous cause, and a sense of political, cultural, and economic helplessness, they turn against the systems of power and resort at least to public protest and social media propaganda, and at worst to physical violence against the offending institution(s). We have seen this most recently in the events of Jan. 6, 2021 in Washington, DC.

This occurs, of course, among the alienated fringes of society, both the far right (more comfortable with violence) and the far left, (to whom the use of violence is not entirely unknown). Just consider certain historical anarchy movements — the Chicago Haymarket Riot and the Weather Underground — not to mention the Black Panther Party.

The paranoid strain has always been with us, but before instantaneous social media, its proponents lived in isolated pockets, unaware of their numbers and potential power to coordinate social disruption. They could feel good about their defiance and their own persecution by the powers that be —

providing a martyr's sense of meaning to their frustrated, confused, and addled minds.

Needless to say, these paranoid citizens will always be able to rationalize their violent actions, and some will never repent their crimes — especially if not confronted by the rule of law and the experience of justice delivered by a proper legal system.

In rhetoric, "antifa" may not be dissimilar to the Proud Boys, but only one group's sense of due process and justice is objectively true and pro-democracy. The other's is essentially fascist.

Keep in mind that on the back of Woody Guthrie's guitar was the inscription, "This instrument kills fascists."

Glossary Addendum:

Early Settlers' fear of the forest: See "Fear and Contempt: A European Concept of Property," by Sidner Larson in *American Indian Quarterly,* Vol. 21, No. 4 (Autumn 1997), pp. 567-577, published by the University of Nebraska Press, https://doi.org/10.2307/1185712.

The Salem Witch Trials: Author Miller's classic *The Crucible* may be the best introduction, especially his preface to the play, revealing just how thoroughly he researched the transcripts of the trials before composing the play. Of course, it was written during the 1950s Second Red Scare McCarthy Senate Hearings exploring Communist influence in the U.S. The Witch Trials were Miller's precedent and metaphor for the political times.

The Anti-Federalists at Constitutional Convention: An excellent primer on the historical importance of the Anti-Federalists at the Constitutional Convention is provided in this blog post by Ugonna Eze, "The Anti-Federalists and their important role during the Ratification fight," Constitution Daily Blog, Sept. 27, 2017, https://constitutioncenter.org/blog/the-anti-federalists-and-their-important-role-during-the-ratification-fight.

The Civil War: Prior to the Civil War, a strong and vocal antislavery movement grew in many states, and there were even activists against slavery in the South. Great Britain had already banned slavery and the South — an agricultural economy too long dependent on slaves — was slow to adapt. The Library of Congress has an excellent web page on Pre-Civil War slavery, "Pre-Civil War African American Slavery." https://www.loc.gov/classroom-materials/united-states-history-primary-source-timeline/national-expansion-and-reform-1815-1880/pre-civil-war-african-american-slavery/

The Chinese Exclusion Act: The National Archives hosts a thorough web page titled "The Chinese Exclusion Act of 1882." The act established a total ban on the immigration of Chinese laborers into the United States. https://www.archives.gov/milestone-documents/chinese-exclusion-act.

The First and Second Red Scares: History.com has a complete treatment of both anti-Communist, hysterical political movements and the ensuing violations of U.S. civil rights. Check out "Red Scare" at https://www.history.com/topics/cold-war/red-scare.

White Citizens' Councils: The Martin Luther King Jr. Research and Educational Institute at Stanford University features a

truly comprehensive website on all aspects of the Civil Rights movement and the secretive organizations of White men working behind the Jim Crow laws that sought to extend oppression.
Visit https://kinginstitute.stanford.edu/encyclopedia/white-citizens-councils-wcc.

The Protocols of the Elders of Zion: This notorious publication is effectively introduced by the U.S. Holocaust Memorial Museum website, "Holocaust Encyclopedia: The Protocols of the Elders of Zion."
https://encyclopedia.ushmm.org/content/en/article/protocols-of-the-elders-of-zion.

The John Birch Society: See Thomas Mallon's "A View from the Fringe: The John Birch Society and the rise of the radical right," *The New Yorker*, Jan. 11, 2016.
https://www.newyorker.com/magazine/2016/01/11/a-view-from-the-fringe.

Ayn Rand: Ayn Rand's philosophy of "Objectivism" is explained efficiently in a two-minute YouTube video developed by the Ayn Rand Institute. Suffice it to say, it glorifies selfishness and disregard of the less fortunate, while claiming to be morally righteous. Jesus may have condemned her to hell. https://www.youtube.com/watch?v=asery3UeBj4 Or just read everything on the Cato Institute web page.

UFO Hysteria: In 2002 *The Guardian* published a report on a study of UFO sightings throughout modern history. The conclusion was that it was a form of "cultural hysteria." https://www.theguardian.com/science/2002/may/05/spaceexploration.research

The Trilateral Commission: Unlike much of the glossary above, the Trilateral Commission actually exists in the real world, much like the Bretton-Woods Agreement, the World Economic Council and the United Nations, all of which seek to promote world peace and economic development in order to prevent future world wars. The paranoia regarding their power (much) and government connections (extensive) is well founded but addle-headed. These people have the most finances to lose; they work cooperatively to NOT kill the goose that lays the golden eggs.

Jonestown Massacre: The History Channel keeps an excellent web page documenting the Jonestown Massacre, and the paranoid theology inspiring the consumption of poisoned Kool-Aid by almost all involved. https://www.history.com/this-day-in-history/mass-suicide-at-jonestown.

Q-Anon: The Southern Poverty Law Center Website keeps a complete treatment of the Q-Anon conspiracy and its anti-social effects in social media and U.S. politics. Suffice it to say, it is the most recent completely paranoid version of the U.S. obsession with imaginary political and social conspiracies. https://www.splcenter.org/hatewatch/2020/10/27/what-you-need-know-about-qanon

Critical Race Theory Political Hysteria: This is a racist reaction to a most excellent explanation of the history of slavery in the U.S. by Professor Nikole Hannah-Jones of Howard University; originally published in the *New York Times* as "The 1619 Project" arguing that U.S. history begins with the dawn of slavery in the "New World."
https://www.nytimes.com/interactive/2019/08/14/magazine/1619-america-slavery.html

Why Progressivism will Triumph Politically — Eventually

Peter Parker, alter-ego of Marvel Comics' Spider-Man, may be best known for his iconic motto: "With great power comes great responsibility." Spider-Man canon attributes the saying to Peter's Uncle Ben. Ignoring the latent paternalism of this sentence, let us take it as a moral truth for this chapter at least.

Stating the obvious, the United States, despite its self-inflicted handicaps, is the wealthiest, most powerful country in world history — by far. Applying the Peter Parker principle, it therefore has greater responsibility than any country today or previous.

These responsibilities exist within its own borders and beyond them to the welfare of less fortunate nations. Yes, this is paternalistic. Yes, it is true. "Feed my sheep," quoth Jesus.

My oldest political memory involves my father, the station wagon, campaign yard signs, a cigar, sledgehammer, and my holding steady a succession of campaign yard signs, supporting Goldwater for president in 1964. I was five. I mentioned this in the Introduction.

In middle school I began rooting for Democratic presidential candidates, beginning with George McGovern. I was one of two students in a class of 30 in Walla Walla, Washington to vote for him in the class mock poll. The two of us were among the few students in the room who had strong interest in national and international issues and policies. Viet Nam was still happening. (As it was spelled in those days.)

My father asked me one evening why I liked the Democrats. My reply, "Dad, you raised me to be a Christian. And Democratic policies are more Christian than Republican ones."

American progressivism was not always a single political party agenda. Early 20th century Republicans like Theodore Roosevelt were enthusiastic advocates of government reform, health and safety in the workplace, and a fair wage for an honest day's work. Roosevelt created the first national park, and fought corporate corruption and monopolistic practices. Appalled by Upton Sinclair's *The Jungle*, he helped establish the first health and safety standards for food and in factories. Prior to his presidency, he was Assistant Secretary of the Navy, when one Friday afternoon while the boss was away, he single-handedly began the Spanish-American War, by ordering Admiral Dewey into Manila Bay to sink the Spain's decrepit Pacific Fleet while it was docked. Not every progressive is nonviolent.

In short, progressives of any party take Peter's uncle at his word.

So does the presidential administration of Joe Biden. During the "Build Back Better" negotiations, certain politicians began to say, "Nobody elected Joe Biden to be FDR." I respectfully disagree. All evidence indicates that the Biden electorate desperately desired a return to progressive values and policies. They want federal activism, they want federal spending, they want increased taxes on the wealthy — these are the same voters who supported Senator Bernie Sanders in the 2016 Democratic primaries. They understand that the issues of today are national issues that require national solutions. The U.S. economy and its pathetic health care system are simply too large and too complex for any one state or a few states to resolve. Every nation of the European Union understands this truth.

From Wilson's "Make the World Safe for Democracy" and his League of Nations initiative, through Teddy Roosevelt's "Square Deal" to FDR's "New Deal," Kennedy's "New Frontier," LBJ's "Great Society," and up to Biden's "Build Back Better," progressives of both parties have worked to peacefully (as far as possible) promote equity and justice in the United States and in international relations.

Elsewhere in this work I introduced the Bretton-Woods International Economic System — yet another gift of American progressivism. We may despise or envy "Davos Man," but these economic leaders keep the relative peace and guarantee relative material wealth.

As the 1999 "Battle in Seattle" took place, I was teaching nearby, south of Seattle in Tacoma, Washington. One of my former students was an organizer. I did not put him up to it. Nor did I encourage another debate student to become chair of the Washington State Libertarian Party. I am an honest political theory broker in the classroom, and never betray my actual values to my students.

Fox News did their best to make this objectivity as difficult as possible, to the point where I was intellectually obligated to say in class that Fox — contrary to their "Fair and Balanced" slogan — was anything but. They preferred to tread the path of Rush Limbaugh — he who received the Presidential Medal of Freedom from then-President Trump (at a State of the Union address, no less). Washington must have rolled over in his grave. I wondered how many previous recipients returned their medals in protest.

Patriotic Economic Political Theorists Deserving of Our Thanks

Shout outs to Paul Krugman, Bernie Sanders, former Labor Secretary and UC Berkeley Professor Robert Reich, and MSNBC's Lawrence O'Donnell. Further thanks to Hans Rosling and his children who finished his essential reading magnum opus: *Factfulness: 10 Reasons We're Wrong About the World and Why Things are Better Than You Think.* I should also throw in Senator Elizabeth Warren, who *should* have been nominated by Democrats for presidential election instead of Hillary Clinton. Warren would have won in 2016.

All the above are most excellent public servants, extremely well educated, personally virtuous, and have a neo-socialist view of where the U.S. needs to go economically to increase equity and social justice. Warren has progressed the most, starting as an Oklahoma youth before her family experienced bankruptcy, prompting her to study economics in college and become a professor specializing in the evaluation of the injustice of bankruptcy law. She has been a thorn in the side of corporate America ever since, God bless her tender soul.

Warren owns a Golden Retriever, Bailey, who appears in her campaign commercials. What's not to love?

Great thanks are due to all these historical and current advocates and protectors of progressivism in the United State of America.

The U.S. population loves Social Security, public education, public transportation, the interstate freeway and highway system, NASA, the U.S. military, the National Park System, the Food and Drug Administration, the Occupational Safety and Health Administration, and the combined museums constituting the Smithsonian, not to mention the U.S. postal system.

All of these are overtly Socialist or Socialist-leaning institutions. FDR stole the idea for Social Security from the Socialist Party of America, who were running against him in 1932, and whose most successful presidential candidate, Eugene V. Debs, received 1,000,000 votes in the 1920 presidential election – while serving a 20-year prison term for opposing the "Great War." Yoda says, "War does not make one great."

My editor says I am conflating Progressivism with Socialism here. I consider them "two sides of the same coin," and the coin is definitely a Euro.

The least the rest of us pikers can do is inform ourselves, study civics and economics, take part in our neighborhood and city governance, and try to, "leave the campsite a little nicer than it was when we arrived."

One of my brothers left that note for the next occupants of our campsite one vacation. The note eventually found its way into a letter to the editor of *The Oregon Journal* written by the campsites' next visitor.

As the bumper sticker says, "Think Globally, Act Locally." I'm starting with this book. Thank you for reading it.

James Matthew Sawatzki: Child number 11 of John and Rosemary of Omaha, Nebraska. They loved each other and their children very much.

Conclusion

Civics is a social construct requiring care and maintenance

As demonstrated in all the essays enclosed, a lack of citizen imagination and will results in continued failure to fix the United States' most pressing and solvable problems — condemning millions to poverty, lack of opportunity, and early death. Meanwhile, Marx's axiom, "The rich grow richer and the poor grow poorer" continues to hold true at the local, state, national and international level. All of it avoidable with a bit of coordinated cooperation by all strata of the body politic.

A simple return to the progressive taxation of the Eisenhower era could provide universal health care; free college education, full employment in construction, infrastructure repair and an end to hunger and poverty.

However, that starts with individuals investing in their own education, and shouldering responsibility for problems they did not create. Benjamin Franklin supposedly quipped to a woman who asked what form of government we would have, "a republic, if you can keep it." Keeping it requires proactive engagement by all affected, with an eye to the Constitution's preamble, "in order to form a more perfect union." This calls not just for voting, but for activism with an eye toward social justice for all.

Jesus wasn't joking when he said, "feed my sheep" or any of his other dozen commandments to engage with fellow planetary citizens, and provide for their needs, regardless of their personal merit. "Whatever you did for one of the least of these brothers and sisters of mine, you did for me." (Matthew 25:40, New International Version)

John Lennon's "Imagine" sets the right tone and calls for reshaping habits of thought, not just changing priorities. I don't particularly care for the atheism of the lyrics. I believe organized religion does far more good than ill in the modern world, although some of our greatest challenges are a legacy of its overwhelming influence in American history — starting with the Puritans and continuing onward toward neo-fascist evangelical Christians, trying to provoke the Second Coming.

Dame Marjorie Chardin in the film *Harold and Maude* reflected, "What use are borders and nations and patriotism?" while later concluding, "Zoos are full, prisons are overflowing; oh my, how the world still dearly loves a cage." Not that there is anything wrong with the promotion of democratic processes across the globe, provided it is done with persuasion and support, and not with the barrel of a gun or an economic iron fist.

Like international currency, nation-states are a legal fiction, *essentially a social construct* useful for exchanging goods and services and for pursuing those goals set forth by the founders in the Constitution: "to form a more perfect Union, establish Justice, insure domestic Tranquility, provide for the common defense, promote the general Welfare, and secure the Blessings of Liberty, to ourselves and our Posterity." All of this is a necessary prerequisite for any form of government, justice system and economy, be it socialist, capitalist or aristocratic.

Rebuilding Germany and Japan, creating the United Nations, implementing the Marshall Plan, and creating a free world economic order via the Bretton Woods Agreement are four of the great philanthropic acts of the modern world. Each was immensely profitable for US corporations – which had not been destroyed in World War II. Sadly, these virtuous behaviors are an exception to U.S. foreign policy, and not always the rule.

Osama bin Laden published an open letter to the United States in November 2002, outlining what the U.S. needed to do to end terrorist attacks, which fairly easily boiled down to two key points: stop supporting corrupts repressive regimes throughout the Middle East, just because they are favorable to your racist, imperialistic and economic hegemony, and reengage with Islamic cultures as economic and political equals.

President John Adams urged restraint in foreign affairs: "We are friends of democracy everywhere, we are defenders of democracy at home." A simple return to such a conservative foreign policy will go a long way to liberating people in other nations, and returning control of our own government to the people governed. At least it is a practical second step.

Finally, citizens need to disengage from that one-eyed monster — social media — which provides the illusion of community to the detriment of the spiritual and economic well-being of all. We must reengage with local, boring administrative political action, the "magisterial offices" Aristotle writes about in *Politics;* school board meetings, election supervision, voter registration, advocating for progressive state initiatives, and testifying at state legislatures when in session.

But most importantly, all citizens must practice personal political virtue, by informing themselves with real newspapers, and promoting the communal good with charity and personal sacrifice. Aristotle posits that there are six forms of government, three virtuous and three corrupt; the virtuous are monarchy, aristocracy and republic; the corrupt forms are tyranny, oligarchy and *democracy*. [*Italics mine.*] Virtuous forms are separated from corrupt forms by the *virtue* of the citizenry.

A perfectly virtuous monarch — a wise old King Arthur — ought to be obeyed by a perfectly virtuous people – chivalrous lords and ladies all. A virtuous elite — like the founding fathers of the U.S. — should be followed by a people who recognize their superiors in virtue, like obedient soldiers under Patton's command ridding Europe of fascism or citizens of India following Gandhi's nonviolence in confronting British imperialism. The unvirtuous forms are all too evident around the globe today, from communist China to Putin's Russia.

But a republic — via its legal constitution (written or otherwise) calls "a warlike multitude" to be more virtuous then is in their nature, allowing them, in service to the greater good, to participate in virtue communally, and improve their virtue in service to the republic.

The rioters of January 6, 2021 were the "warlike multitude," and their leaders, "the most unvirtuous of men" in recent American history. They all need to read this work, and work on themselves.

Go forth, and serve others, in service to yourself. It's the only way to "keep the republic."

73